Tapping At Glass
Tim Tim Cheng

VERVE
POETRY PRESS
BIRMINGHAM

PUBLISHED BY VERVE POETRY PRESS
https://vervepoetrypress.com
mail@vervepoetrypress.com

FIRST PUBLISHED FEB 2023 / REPRINTED NOV 23

Printed and bound in the UK
by Imprint Digital, Exeter

ISBN: 978-1-913917-29-6

CONTENTS

Notes & Acknowledgements

Tapping At Glass

Bathtub

The most pressing question today
is why your head
fits right onto my shoulder.

The rest is *soap! soap! soap!*

Like the earth, I become hotter and hotter.

(I starfished in your bed last night, you said.)

Have you seen one of those square starfish?
They look like a fucking wallet!

What's star-shaped anyway?
You can't outline explosions, can you?

(I pushed you out of bed, you said.)

Sounds like your problem.

Icarus, a girl, talks to interviewers

*after The New York Times' feature on the second
Chinese female astronaut*

You asked if I was afraid of the sun
melting my eye makeup.
I had waxed enough to know beauty burned
and some places were better left
untouched—questions, like ingrown hairs,
trapped under the skin in the wrong direction.
My father named me after my brother
but never made me wings, not wanting
to admit to his own misjudgement:
I did listen, and I flew better—oh the solitude
I had, not being father's favourite son,
too loud, had Chang'e not been writing back.

The sun was too bright for my taste.
I packed my makeup (but not sanitary products)
and waited for the moon to wax,
its murmur tickling my nape. Of Chang'e's
many stories, I knew she drank
her husband's elixir to fly to the moon
just to escape the celebration sex
after he shot down those nine damned suns.
You thought she was running away
from domesticity. Did you ask her husband
to water their osmanthus tree,
or if eyeliners helped him aim better?

No. So why did you act shocked
as I ascended? Accuse Chang'e and I
for deviance. We no longer need
the safety of your approval. Now:
my skirt, opening upwards;
my breasts, anti-gravitational;
the stars; the glitter on my eyes,
free from your orbitary gaze. On a lucky day,
when the moon is red from the beads
floating around me, some of which
spatter in your face, you'll know
I've shed your ill-fitting space suit.

Beds

after Fili Papinho's flower embroidery

My back and mattress form an inexact line,
a horizon refusing light. I turn for my peace lilies.
In half-shade, their lush, glossy green
slouches like silence.
     They may as well wilt for the thought of wetness,
rising as soon as I water them again, arriving home
from a one-night stand, forever distracted
by others' arrhythmical plants.
       Call this feeling seasonal—
what controls me makes me too—black threads
tie my limbs to a false lily's flowers, stitching me
into its wide white spathe.
     I am in my underwear.
My legs, lopsided hills. Way-laid, I look away
from the lily's damp softness. Its rim singes,
a stillness ringing
    I will, I will, I will—
just not now: the lilies in my room are curling in,
shrouding their sexes. I have not killed them, have I—
I behead them to return them to soil.
      Where water passes,
a darker shade over their veined papery grasp.

SHE WILL
after the film Shell *(2012) by Scott Graham*

A car crash is just touching
too much—the father
scurries into the headlight
like the roadkill he butchers, the meat
his daughter cooks reluctantly.
    Shock is when you eat
and bite into the membrane
of your lips instead—the daughter
darts from his bed, bruised
like whatever fruit her body isn't.
    You, lit-up by your screen,
choke up on the daughter's cry:
how stories are the last refuge
of mistakes. Things unwanted in life
could just live there. The father,
the daughter, shelled in their motherless wild,
take turns to push each other's
kisses away—they do what they do
to show you how far
things could carry over.
    But what about the day,
just that one day your father
cries, telling you things
you think only your mother
should know. He edges too close
by your bed. His temperature,
an omen. The ear you lend him
forcibly opened. Your panic
is a burst kitchen pipe
your father fails to stop—
    you escape for the first time,
wearing a plain, white shirt,
wondering if you're mistaken
for your mother. You live inside a hotel
mirror. This man, another man
you barely know, whose hands run all over
your insecurities, is sound asleep
like a foetus—how do you tell
what is and what isn't until
    you watch the daughter outrun her past.

Boyfriend for Scale
after Maggie Smith's 'Wife for Scale'

History is wild grass peeking out
through earth-coloured ruins—

tourists gather like toothache
at the mouth of old traps,

the spikes of which are rusty
from search dogs and enemies.

The always-retiring tour guide asks us
to pose next to a phallic statue.

He looks at me, smirking.
What does this stone look like?

We're the last interracial couple he asks,
as if he wants to be entertained too.

It is and is not a lie when I say
a thumbs-up magnified. A photo I take

does show you raising your thumb
by the rock, which is your size.

Tell me: if I said *it's a human-sized dick,
just like you* to the tour guide,

would that make us sacrilegious
but honest? When he asks you, not me,

if we are engaged or married,
you say *yes*

to him because I also agree
that's more convenient. Does that read

it's inconvenient to be me—
too young, too female

and too Asian? Forgive me, I am letting
history talk over my heartache—

next to souvenir stalls, we are sick of
the millionth photo of one important leader

shaking hands with other important leaders.
We stop holding hands too.

Beginner's Wall, Shek O

Big waves lick boulders above the sea level.
    A typhoon brought salt, now ashy,
over volcanic cliffs, where we sit.
    We pick up small pieces of graphite,
trailing our spot to prove their colouration.
    I lie like seaweed drying for consumption,
arms stretched next to my ears, and stare
    at the sky wide open, seamless with the sea,
a gradient of indigo and turquoise where
    ribbons of sand and foam intersperse.
If you look hard enough, waves from afar
    carry incessant gouges like woodcut.

A challenge I can't take without liquid courage:
    rock-climbers set ropes, fix harnesses
and check helmets for each other, trusting
    their weight with muscle strength and grip.
Giving in to gravity, too, is sometimes crucial.
    Let hips sink onto an invisible chair mid-air
for rest. The hard part is to know you won't fall.
    Tension! Tension! Climbers' partners
on the ground look up for commands. The language
    one must learn facing speechless crags.
The wind growls, uncritical to recent histories
    of survival out of besieged brick walls.

Clouds and Clouds

the air is not warring
but we are

        gathering at billboards
        where half-cleaned slogans

pass through us
clouds are monuments

        floating into our rooms
        a blur   a lifetime

I am breathing in
the streets   acrid tarmac

        fills my lungs
        parks would be nice

bushes smell of smoke
tear gas is an ice-cream flavour

        everything melts   my hands
        glass powder   burns my throat and eyes

winds disperse   smoulders
traces   reach too far

        but sometimes they hide us
        from cops   from being known

behind a fence
white and shapeless

        we run   I can't see who
        give me goggles

we are as scarred   as our city
as the sky   withholds its clues

        I look out   a smog
        the size of our war cries

Shockproof
Sai Kung

There are so many ways of breaking: in one,
he cried on my shoulder, hearing
how mending teenage bones, fractured
by a certain gravity the night before,
would take too many nails and years; in one,
everyone asked if he could
fill the breakage in household items
with lacquer and metal powder,
overlooking the burn before all that
golden joinery; in one, we went to the fringe
of the city, despite the city, to see
the work of earth movements tower
by the rolling sea: hexagonal basalt columns
given rise by the uniform contraction
of lava gushing, then cooling
in seabed depression a billion years ago.

Rocks, sacrifices and songs—*I love you
twisted. I love you straight.* I'm aware
there're so many ways of breaking. They don't
always lead to magnificence. In one,
it doesn't matter if we could tell stitches
and forensic underscores apart; in one,
it does. We've broken the seismic silence
to the point where we know more
than what's not told. I'm not asking
if their breaking counts as mine. I'm not
a baby needing elder's protection, like,
a loop of jade that shatters against evil
or a silver necklace that turns black
absorbing fever. I know too well that only
my own unmaking can save me.
I'm just a little less than shockproof.

Topography
Outbound from Lai Chi Wo

We discerned waves drenched in sunset
as our ferry dragged across the water.

The twelve of them are somewhere over there
He pointed to an expanse far north—

Yantian, Salt Field, a name on the map
of no escape, of letters to and fro

an unseen prison everywhere, nowhere.
I mouthed their names to myself

out of the fear of forgetting, as I might have
without those clear, vertical name cards

coincidentally released the same day.
(The mind does filter for daily functions.)

In the same water of the twelve's arrest,
there's no building but a police fleet

to which we gave the finger briefly
in the safety of our ferry. It navigated

by mossy bumps, enormous, small,
pointy, or round, all labelled in the same map.

Their strange names rolled in mind:
Wu Lei Kiu, Mai Fen Tsui, Ngau Si Buut,

Lan Tau Pai (Fox-Cry; Rice Noodle Mouth;
Dung Alms Bowl; Rotten Head Platoon)

Their contours never quite mattered
until I searched for something to hold onto.

How Memory Works

on the closure of Apple Daily, the biggest pro-democracy press in Hong Kong

i.

We see the newspaper for tomorrow, not tomorrow
It's already midnight. Today that is. News that stays
warm and inky on our fingertips at 2:30 am.

ii.

I keep thinking of a *kong girl* last year this time,
one among the thousands staying up to queue,
to stream: her black T-shirt, hot pants, flip flops.

iii.

Printers rumble and spit beyond the usual volume.
Papers snake along conveyor belts, up and down,
all over the factory. The ASMR of holding fast.

iv.

Sure they won't catch us for buying the paper?
Mother went with me, still. She prayed for me
to hear before the elevator. Ghosts police too.

v.

I would love to believe the sky
is apologising but it never does.
We rain on its behalf.

vi.

In convenience stores:
Cashier A: "It's not here yet" without looking.
Cashier B: "How many copies?" without counting.

vii.

Newspapers are a genre for fathers.
They die again with the newspaper.
Their absence, the absence of words

viii.

Tat Ming Pair: *why is this person making
me ask for the only choice in this garden?*
I picked a formless fruit, already forbidden.

ix.

Windowless: news about news. Bars behind bars.
Forms of Farewell: stare straight. Hit and miss.
Sounds and fury. Refresh—404 not found.

x.

We saved interviews and unphotogenic snaps,
the mean, low-cost animations too.
We mourn every day. We are good at it now.

Reiki

for Pamela and 我地張家

I sat next to Pamela, waiting
for our friends to call it a day,

for the Mihn club to open.
She put her palms together

and barely blinked, focused
on somewhere beyond

the shop window. Outside,
the dark alley a mirror:

I asked if she was meditating.
She said no and lifted one hand—

a card, written with names: the couple's,
(their cat's too) and the hospital's.

She invited me to place my palm
in the space between hers.

"I'm sending energy to the wife.
She's due tomorrow and she's so

tiny... you know." "I know...
been following the husband's

letters from the prison."
My shoulders loosened in the warmth.

I stopped talking to make room,
thinking of an infant's playdough fist

tight around a mother's finger,
insulated by a big wish.

News, Nocturnal

i.

Tonight I see things that look, from afar, like fireflies.
Flashlights on phones sway in an auditorium
to the last slow tune. A singer tells us: *we don't just scream*
for suffering tonight. It's liberating, too. We release

the wolves and thunderclaps within us.

                              I come home
to a video of a tree-rimmed, roaring night sky.
A man exclaims behind the camera, in Arabic,
as orange sparks streak overhead: stamens and pistils
without flowers. Flickers bloom at each other,

the sound of someone tapping at glass.

ii.

        Weeks later, slowly,

Raja Shehadeh's book calls me from my old shelf.
I read it at work. I read it before sleep
to the shouts of protests, smaller, unstopped,

more harmless than the ones before.

> *We still sit under an olive tree*
> *in the quiet valley*
> *of the occupied land*
> *to watch the light and shadows take turns.*

His words swim off my vision like floaters,
like the emoji confetti we share among ourselves
for the news we live in. We share and share
to the edge of awareness, where noises may flare
into voices, voices into a good world—but for now, this dark
is just dark, a din. Lead us
                        through the echos
to each other.

Since Marina and Grace brought me white roses

I couldn't stop playing my favourite song,
same-titled as the flowers, from thirteen years ago.
I stored the roses in cheap wine bottles

I never recycled. They might be from the same Tesco,
finally meeting at my table.

Tikhanovsky jailed for 18 years over protests—
Canto-pop star Eason Chan cuts ties with Adidas
after it rejects Xinjiang cotton—

Headlines fell from our mouths.
I could hear the clink of our speech and teeth

being shaken in our mugs.
When we hugged each other goodbye,
Belarus, London, and Hong Kong touched.

I looked at the roses and put my headphones on.
The song turned my insides into cotton.

White like white moth, white fang—
White like white sugar, white fuss—
A lyricist was whited out by order, too.

How do I boycott a singer from his song
when tonight, it speaks to me again?

Have I lost the language of softness
or is this how fuzzy it is
between being good and authentic?

I thought of Eileen Chang, who inspired the song
who was said to laugh during sex,

whose landlord found her dead
alone in her Californian apartment;
and the singer, and me, nostalgic

for a country of small comfort.

NOTES TO IMPOSSIBILITY

Where I come from, everyone is free
to exercise their freedom loudly
once. I want to do it well.

It'd really suck if bad arts got us
into trouble. Stuck
with a banned thing
that we hated. My friend and I
laugh about this and for a moment,
the walls aren't listening.

We live well, at least we try—
I do my dishes by hand
to get a little closer to the river.
I stare at my first pot of lilies
and bloom into the child I wasn't.
I reply to my family more,
begging with trees
to rake the wind still, the way

my great granny kept dying
until she didn't. What shocked me more
was how a call from the hospital
could excuse me from work right away.

How freeing grief is—
I never sweep my family's tombs
but pace through public memorials
to cry with crowds I've never met.

It takes a whole world to burn
me into someone I might believe in,
knowing utter hope and despair
comes from the same pride
that can't free itself from itself.

The only correct analogy
between a city and your family
is when there's no return
but you still dream of home.

Field Notes
North East New Territories, Hong Kong

FROM THE SOIL

We make our son. From the soil we make our son biscuits. From the soil we make our son biscuits stored in ceramic bowls. From the soil we make our son biscuits stored in ceramic bowls made with the same soil. From the soil we make our son biscuits stored in ceramic bowls made with the same soil we dig, burn, grind into red dusts. From the soil we make our son biscuits stored in ceramic bowls made with the same soil we dig, burn, grind into *red dusts*, which means *earthly affairs*, a dream in an utterance that presupposes us.

DAY TRIPS

Your son tugs at my sleeve, making me get him the red sugar cubes you prepared for our tea. Zest and mint. He knows I'm eager to please but you notice. So you push away the red sugar cubes and give him biscuits instead. The biscuits look like tiny pebbles. "These are sweet too." Tiny fingers. Tiny bites. He is always eating. The way he abandoned his bread in the bookshelf for play last time we visited. This farm, this house, his birthplace: layered red soil, ghosts, and labour in the bathtub. Sweet when taken in small doses.

GIVE AND TAKE

Take the mugwort and rub it on your skin. Take the lemongrass spray. The bugs are used to us. We are used to the bugs. They could tell you are new here so they go at you. Take the tomatoes. It's not a harvest, it's an explosion from the unbroken rain. I have been eating them, *only* eating them for a week. Take the white corn. Eat them raw. A burst of sunshine. Take Luk Sum. Take Man Gor. Take Ling Tai. Take Fai Gei. Take Tong San. Take Ling Jie. Take other farmers in mind, too. Oh, don't forget the last batch of tofu from a friend's closing factory.

STRANGENESS

The potatoes I take home are tiny and firm, except for one. Rinsing the potato, I poke my finger through the mud-filled holes, scared of any sign of life inside. The mud crumbles into more mud. A hollowed-out starch maze. A sign that the earth does not taste metallic. I often think I could farm, except for the snakes that slither into village houses, except for finishing the day's work before the scathing noon. Sometimes, life stops changing for the smallest of reasons, such as not being able to wake up with the sun.

TRUST

"Our son was born before dawn. We named him Hei Yeung, *hope for the sun*. I never quite trusted the hospital. We read and discussed with each other to decide on the bathtub. The what-ifs became shared. Not all of us agreed. The ones who stayed in the farmhouse helped my home birth." "We do talk about everything, like the way we share our income: wage or taking from the communal safe when needed?" "Sometimes we lose friends with the same belief, who want it differently." "But I know they're out there, working."

TO YIELD

Serve—sever; our—out: gunshots from unseen barracks puncture the air. Some doors do not open in the village, not just these vintage cars before us but always the fire, always the bulldozer razing the soil before it is taken from your hands. Farmers without farms. The city that no longer feeds itself collapses into your throat. "My tears sell better than my crops, eh?" Your mind, your body yields to the soil, despite—the day a friend's farm shuts down, another celebrates a tiny harvest. Rice stalks bend slightly in giving.

Salt and Rice

between a Cantonese father and daughter, 2020

How much salt have you eaten over the years,
to make you always state the opposite
with a grain of salt? How many grains of salt
do you need to fill up your *salt shakers*,
your *dignity*? Does your daily dignity lie
in how you *have had more salt than my having rice?*
You can't eat democracy like rice,
you said, *hands stop, mouth stops*, a job is a job.
Can you still translate a day job as *find eat*
if you are skipping lunch for work? If work
can't guarantee *safety, joy, tea and rice*, why
shouldn't we rise? *We, rise?* Do *we* really
read as *everyone*? Some do prefer rolling
as salt in waves to being crystallised.

Boxed in

I could find anything but mooncakes or cookies
in those rusty tin boxes under the sofa:
bills and keys, needles and threads, pirated porn
in flimsy plastic packages with low-res covers.

Once, dad locked mum and me out—mad,
because granny stole his VCDs, saying
they were unhealthy for the family.
She consumed them alone at her own place.

I'd often thought dad was watching porn, too,
in the next room, and almost told him about the
local websites that offered more than pixelated genitals.
He deserved better viewing experiences for his hard

work. He did find out, years into smartphones.
He looked nervous when he realised he'd forgotten
about all the tabs before lending me his tablet, which I
closed without a word before he snatched it back.

(H)ours

Find one with a marble-clad lobby
where Venus without arms stands.
We are looking for taste and quality.
Don't you dig the woman and man
entwined into a face of gold lines
on a black canvas on the lift's wall?
It's always lovely to have artwork at our back.
It'd have been better, though,
if the bedroom came with a window.
But in the meantime it won't really hurt,
we've stopped expecting the freedom of a bird.

The walls of this district are plastered
with impossible prices of apartments.
But if one can't buy one,
splitting, sponsoring, borrowing,
or subdividing hourly, weekly, monthly
may help one get some.
Who said the young don't plan ahead,
or the old are all settled?
This place lets in diversities
of customers, purposes, and rooms.

Oh look, this bathroom's surely spacious
for most private activities, and it's considerate indeed
to equip the room with monkey picked oolong
and condoms dependent on how long
we will stay.

In and Out

Mrs Wong's microphone wasn't working.

She plugged and unplugged the thing,
while maintaining her phonetic teaching
in textbook standard clarity:
In. Out. In. Out. In. Out. In.
Oh. it's out of order—

Her gold-rimmed glasses
are low hanging as her breasts,
which shall be tucked inside
socks for staying warm.

Mostly I hated her
for calling me out one recess
from the basketball court, asking
if I was *bad at other subjects, too,*
aside from English. I should,
she said, *avoid bad influences*
since they're all smarter than me.

I still think about Mrs Wong
when I look at my breasts;
when people ask if I write
in Cantonese besides English;
or when I teach vowels
with apologies to my students,
who endure my demonstration,
those *ah, ah, ah, ah, oh, oh, oh.*

Mrs Wong might not remember me
but she is always watching
my inner teenage boy,
who is neither good nor bad,
always sprawling from a period
like a question mark.

The Tattooist

I let my friends' children ink my back,
a noisy, wild mess, somewhere between
a playground and a bar's toilet.

A boy slashed a drooping penis here,
you see, slightly below my shoulder blade.

He used to doodle erections everywhere:
his family's house, his school's wall,
his own assignments, my sketchbook
although we'd just met.

So I told him, *vandalise me*
with an actual tattoo gun.

His eyes were wide, hands shaky
as he stabbed the machine
into my back, forging confidence.

It was his first flaccid penis,
and the last he drew in public.

Froggos, Froggone

Shui Hau

Tonight you're not dried and flat,
blending into the road.
You croak like no one's watching,
loud, multiple—

among you, there's this ridiculous laughter,
surround sound of *abracadabra, abracadabra,*
distinct, almost like a mockery
to the itchy fact
that our blood is your food's food
by the thick, green soup
of your lotus leaves and children,
some of which will never grow.

We thought you were extinct
and how the hell did you return—

Our flashlight gives no answer
but to reveal
you, stoic, resting on bark
or under a big grass blade;
you, so many of you
looking out from drain pipes;
or swept into a gutter
higher than you could leap—

so we cup our hands to take you
back to the wet bush,
by which you freeze,
unblinking, as if
making sense
of the tunnelling, of gods' hands
before you turn left then right
then spring out of sight.

Waterlogged

from Hong Kong to Edinburgh

Cloud puffs hovered below,
their shadows above red tile roofs.
Vapour condensed on double-paned windows,
straining to contain
the bird's eye view of everything,
faintly outlined in my English books.

The limbo of a long haul
muffled my fear for other passengers' droplets.
Pass me the wine. Spill the tea
at the slightest of turbulence.
I'd never noticed how dry the air
in the cabin was until then,

two years since not flying. Last time I flew,
Mount Fuji stood constant in dense clouds
at the dawn of news back home.
I never knew how much rain the sky
and a person could hold. Perhaps,
I never will. If I were to make this place

my home, this language I've lived
outside but scratched at,
would the news back home get old?
The day I landed, there's a sudden shower
in the sun. The city greeted me:
raindrops in a stranger's copper hair.

intertidal

the sun is a white blur in water   pulsing   pulsing
     as currents   cut stretch marks   in sand
light travels   along sheer veins   sequins
     past algae and kelps   bundled   sprawling
        wavy   at rest   I salivate   at sea-spray
     (should've brought   vinegar and garlic)
        all these sea vegetables   some dried   exposed
     among rocks   scarred by motions
a small spiral   spins open   this wrinkly translucence

~

        across a black-winged beach   that island
is a blunt stroke in haze   rising slightly before its cliff
     where memory seems   world-less
       If I jumped   would I forgive   myself
    for leaving   what would   catch me
rocks laddered   creased   like faces
     hummocks raw   like dough   or waves rushing
       towards themselves   A person is walking his dog
     slight shadows   such brightness

~

the path up this green disc   of an island   only appears
     at low tide   moisture oozes   with every step
       boulders   pebbles   are maps
     pressed together   by centuries   some salt-rimmed
barnacled contours   resemble burns   overgrown terrains
     holding small lakes   I walk closer   to the soft edge
of this grassy crag   as far   as my legs won't quiver
     I can't tell   where   the atlantic and north sea meet
The wind   dispels nations   inside me

Horrible Kids

Was thinking of flowers in boots
by Orkney's clear shore   and scampi to be had
in my hotel room   Two white pre-teens
passed by   holding an ice-cream

and coughed   and coughed

Took me a few seconds
to turn back   They looked at me

and laughed

Took me a few seconds I just
walked faster   and   told my friends online
about what might have been

racism   a double pandemic

My friends asked why   I didn't
throw a brick   or shout at them
or fake louder coughs

Took me a few seconds
to recall   a Pakistani mother
who screamed at me in Cantonese
in a park back in Hong Kong

when I wondered aloud
that her kid   *could also speak Cantonese?!?!*

I was a horrible kid   too
didn't understand her fury   until now

I am glad   she yelled

How Do You Spell [   ] in Chinese
after Susie Dent's tweet on the etymology of the word 'trees'

I hug trees with my languages. Those slow bodies of truth. I kiss books that simmer in action. Some words kiss me back.

A teacher said ideograms are often stories. When vision dims at

> [sunset 夕],
>> a name 名字 comes out of your mouth 口.

At birth,

> [words 字]
>> arrive like a rooftop 宀 for the child 子.

If the sun is too bright

> [to read 看],
>> you use your hand 手 to shelter your eyes 目.

Some creation myths are lost on me though:

> [one who...者]
>> extends from juicing sugar canes.

Who acts out of sweetness now? What if words sweep me away more often than housing me? Can't we just stay close enough we don't need to call each other? Speaking of things my hands can do...

I don't need such figments now. I'm busy thinking about the sugar cane juice we had in Vietnam, the freshest from a street vendor you didn't trust.

Before I met you, language had never been this visceral. When you are gone, I grow inwards like bark, losing myself in the library of everything.

I knew time never lost track of me the night I read *Six Walks in the Fictional Woods*. In a planetarium, Eco watched a recording of the night sky during his birth. He thought it was the best origin story one could die in.

I looked out the window from our cross-city sleeper bus. Beyond my upper bunk bed parallel yours, stars were unnumbered—like the dandruff on your punk t-shirts—above dense, dark trees.

Ars Poetica with Translations

after Alycia Pirmohamed

The poet says gwong si, *light is, this alone.*

Say *this alone could make light*
of you.

You empty your laundry basket and think—
pour socks, poet—
dou mat si yan
see things miss you

In a translation, you never learn
object permanence.
Missing someone doesn't remind you
of death. You laugh
like infants playing peekaboo.

The poet makes a sound, si,
that bends nine times at least: a *poem*
is a *body* is a *history* is a *test*
is *time, markets, matter, sensualities,*
tin, kisses, food...

In a translation, the 詩人 insists
on the full 私隱
of their first tongues, like rocks
against currents.

The poet baths in the tonal spectrum
where *brilliance* and *sadness*
are not far.

NO LANGUAGE

Imagine dipping Indomie onto your black hair dye and imprint it on paper like a doctor's prescription: would you enjoy it the way you laugh reading a tabloid upside down? I did not pay attention. We were taught to ignore who you were. Granny didn't think it could help us settle down in Hong Kong. Had you been the mutable Pisces according to your birth date, before you were great-granny? Had your life been intelligible to yourself, a maid sold to a Fujian landlord? Learned by ears for survival, your mix of Hokkien, Mandarin, Cantonese, Indonesian, and simple English was not something I was proud of, until I met Umberto Eco's Salvatore, who *speaks all languages, thus no language*. I just wanted the McDonald's staff to understand your order. Did it make a difference when the stroke took away your speech? I didn't know what to do by your sickbed until a pet-loving cousin tickled you on the side you still felt, saying *or bi shi tung mai. dak shawe bu lu el* in our horrible Cantonese accent. Were you thinking of the ducks you slaughtered for your hungry daughter when you rolled your eyes, grunting disapproval? I wish I knew you other than being a food provider. I wish we had another portrait for your funeral, not the grainy one enlarged from your I.D. card, where waves swam officially over your tight lips and your havoc of short curls in artificial black.

Self-Portrait of My Granny in the Voice of Anti-Japanese Drama's Protagonists

I, full of passion and education,
was trained in martial arts. I could jump high—
up to the sixth floor. I loved my nation
despite having five passports. You asked why
I couldn't handle my grandchild's homework
and never moved to another country.
The point is, the Japanese are the worst.
It's true, the show, our soldiers fought bravely.
With bare hands, we could halve our enemy.
Yes, I was sent to farms during uni.
Yes, dad gave up his land to dodge assaults
but Mao zhuxi's deeds did outweigh his faults.
 I miss you. I'm glad you're back to see me.
 Do you want some of these salmon sushi?

Kindergarten

i.

Granny did my homework—I cried
copying the alphabets
in my exercise book: capital letters
must touch the top and bottom red lines
while small letters must stay
between the blue lines.

The only English granny knew was
how do you do-do. i luffu yiu
but she wanted to save me from the pain.
She flipped over my exercise book
to follow the exemplary, new shapes
of a language more valued
than her, under the laced, intricate table
of the Chinese multiplication song.

Her hand-writing was rounder,
steadier than mine.
My teacher seemed to know
but she was angrier at the fact that
we copied with coloured pencils:
every letter was a blunt rainbow
just because there's no pencil
nor sharpener in our household.

ii.

Every new school year started with a new
English name: the class monitor took
Mary, name of the main girl in our book.

My teacher said *Tim Tim, you could take
Cindy from Cinderella. She's a princess.*

I liked it although it didn't occur to me
that the said princess was 灰姑娘, Miss Grey,
for who I knew the Chinese name.

I went home and told granny about this.
She asked, *what would my English name be?*
Your cheeks are red. You must be an Apple!

Granny liked this. Years on, she still repeats:
Halo, how do you do-do? My name is Apple!

Sonnet with Skylines
after Cynthia Miller's Sonnet with Lighthouses

The first skyline is my grandmother.

The second is her silver front tooth.

The third is foam. I open her window frame, climb onto the balcony and clean the glass. Sometimes I pick up her old laundry, and I look down and out.

The fourth skyline is invisible. I have always lived on the first floor.

The fifth is shy, folding itself over and over on my neighbour's windows. Some households are ice-cubes. White approaches purple approaching green.

My name is not written into the sixth skyline: a blazing web of roads jewelled by lampposts. Estates from afar sheen like coins in a safe.

The seventh is always thirsty.

The eighth wells up.

The ninth is a photo of Victoria Harbour on a clear day erected in front of the actual harbour in smog. The Tourism Board manifests itself.

Stumbling   into the tenth skyline   my friends and I   drink it dry   Cheap leather and
shisha stick   like second skin   We lie by the waterfront   There is no one else
No flashes in red and black   No office light   Just the sun entering glass panes

The eleventh is crumpled and stuffed into the mouths of those who, by harboring Hong Kong, overtake.

The twelfth expands like brass notes, like love.

The thirteenth knows I am my own stereotype. I take an old friend to Garden Hill, where I identify as a giant stray cat. Highrises are shoebox stairs teeming with light. Around us, every leaf is a cicada. Their silhouettes are louder than cars. When he says he loves my city, I cut his outline from it, thinking I might be good enough for him too.

The fourteenth skyline plays hide-and-seek, never found.

NOTES

1. 'Since Marina and Grace brought me white roses,' contains news headlines from BBC and Hong Kong Free Press, as well as lyrics by Francis Lee, who took inspiration from Eileen Chang, a novelist whose life was subject to analysis and rumours. A month before the release of this pamphlet, Eason Chan hinted at Xinjiang cotton in his concert with an ambiguous lightheartedness, which stirred discussions on his online statement in the previous year. I thought this poem, like many immediate political reactions, might have expired by the turn of events.

2. 'Icarus, a girl, talks to interviewers' is a response to questions interviewers asked the second Chinese female astronaut, such as: "do you need to wear a bra in outer space?"

3. 'Waterlogged' records my two flight experiences, one on 21 July 2019, another on 9 September 2021. The former date is remembered as 'the 721 mob attack', which marked the watershed of Hong Kong's Anti-extradition protests.

4. 'Beginner's Wall, Shek O' is set after several university sieges in Hong Kong that took place in November 2019. Protesters who occupied university campuses were confronted by the police. Some protesters escaped by means of abseiling and pipe climbing. Speculations and lawsuits ensued. Writing this in the past tense feels strange because trials are still ongoing. Civilians are kept in custody indefinitely, too.

5. 'News, Nocturnal' contains my (re-)translation of the Chinese version of *Palestinian Walks: Notes on a Vanishing Landscape* by Raja Shehadeh. The Chinese translators are 馬永波 and 楊于軍.

6. 'Clouds and Clouds' comes from a workshop titled 'On Forensic Architecture' with Dr Samaneh Moafi, which was organised by Scottish BPOC Writers Network.

7. 'Shockproof' contains a line from the song '15 Petals' covered by Jamie N Commons; 'How Memories Work', my translation of Tat Ming Pair's '每日一禁果'.

8. 'Self-Portrait of My Granny in the Voice of Anti-Japanese Drama's Protagonists' takes inspiration from China's television dramas, some of which re-tell the wars between China and Japan in the 20th century in order to instil nationalistic feelings.

9. 'Salt and Rice''s last line alludes to 海浪裏的鹽：香港九十後世代訪談故事 by 蔡寶賢, which is a book that compiles interviews of people who were born in the 1990s. The poem is mostly made of Cantonese idioms directly translated into English.

10. 'How do you spell [   ] in Chinese' gets its title from the common misunderstanding that Chinese could be spelt like English. I might have not gone beyond Erza Pound's extraction of Chinese radicals.

11. 'Ars Poetica with Translations' plays with homophones and the tonal differences of Cantonese words. This poem is an imaginative exercise of puns and linguistic coincidences in Cantonese rather than an accurate description of the thought system(s) it embodies.

ACKNOWLEDGEMENTS

This book would not have existed without May Fung, Ms Choy, Sigrid Tang, my parents, and my grandmother, who supported my study at The University of Edinburgh, where learning and friendships from the MSc in Creative Writing (Class of 2022) have changed me. I will not be sick of saying your names: Medha Singh, Olivia Thomakos, Amy Curtis, Liam Wright, Shelby Schumacher, Heather Dunnett, Han Le, and Tamara Raidt. Thank you, Scottish BPOC Writers Network, for the constant inspirations and safe space with cookies. Thank you, Tammy Lai-Ming Ho, Miriam Gamble, Alan Gillis, Patrick James Errington, Niall Campbell, Jennifer Wong, Ruth Hung, Lian-hee Wee, Jason Eng Hun Lee, Jason S Polly, James Shea, and Ryan Van Winkle for teaching me how to love words. Thank you, Collier Nogues, Nicholas Wong, Alvin Pang, Louise Leung, Felix Chow, Helena Wong, Kwok Tsz Ki, Au Wahyan, L. Kiew, WrICE 2021 fellows, and Bereket Writing Community for believing in me before I could. Thank you, Karen Cheung, for writing about Hong Kong's subcultures in English when not many were. Thank you, William Ng, Adin Chu, Jimmy Chan, Grace Wong Hiu-yan, Zabrina Lo, and many more, who suffered during my undergraduate-poet phase. Thank you, my (the audacity of possessive pronouns!) previous students and coworkers, who made me realise that perfection is nothing without the joy of creation. Thank you Wai Ching, Ka-yu, Charlie Yu Ling, Choihung Mingki, Zi, Miki, Freddie, and my flatmates from Hong Kong to Tartu to Edinburgh, for reality checks and emotional support. Thank you, Max, for being your utmost Virgo self by disproving astrology. Thank you, Hongkongers, for all the moments we share, without which I would not know it is normal to have feelings. Thank you, poetry, for helping me stay in touch with myself, and with the terrible beauty we call this world. I will shrug it off with a joke and avoid eye contact in person but here it is: THANK YOU for the love. I do not know how to handle this.

My heartfelt gratitude, too, to the editors and/or organisers of the following avenues. Your trust and/or advice on the earlier versions of my poems are invaluable. 'SHE WILL' appeared in *Grierson Verse Prize*; 'Icarus, a girl, talks to interviewers' and 'The Tattooist' in *AMNLY*; 'Beginner's Wall, Shek O' in *Oxford Poetry Brookes Centre* and *Berfrois*; 'Shockproof' and 'Topography' in *Cicada*; 'How Memory Works' in *The Commons*; 'Salt and Rice' in *Rabbit Poetry Journal*; 'NO LANGUAGE' in *harana*; 'Boxed in' in *Sine Theta Magazine*; '(H)ours' in *Voice and Verse Magazine*; 'Kindergarten' in *Parenthesis journal*; 'NOTES TO IMPOSSIBILITY' in *The Rialto*; 'Field Notes' in *POETRY*; 'Froggos, Froggone' in *Asia Art Archive*; 'Horrible Kids' in *Tupelo Quarterly*; ' Waterlogged' and 'intertidal' in *Our Time is a Garden*; 'intertidal' in *The Nature Library (Ullapool)*; 'In and Out' in *Interpret*; 'Boyfriend for Scale' in *Under the Radar*; 'How Do You Spell [   ] in Chinese' in *Propel*; 'Sonnet with Skylines' in *The Oxonian Review*; 'Reiki' in *Canto Cutie*.

ABOUT THE AUTHOR

Tim Tim Cheng is a poet and teacher from Hong Kong, currently based between Edinburgh and London. Her poems are published or anthologised in *POETRY, The Rialto, Ambit, Cicada, Our Time is a Garden*, and elsewhere. She has spoken in transnational literary panels across Asia-Pacific regions, the States, and the UK. Her latest appearances include the Hidden Door festival, and Loop, BBC Scotland. Named 'one of the seven female poets to know in Hong Kong' by *Tatler Asia*, she is also a William Hunter Sharpe Memorial Scholarship awardee, WRiCE fellow, Roddy Lumsden Memorial Mentorship mentee, and a member of the Southbank Centre New Poets Collective. She tranlates, edits, and writes ltrics. timtimcheng.com

ABOUT VERVE POETRY PRESS

Verve Poetry Press is a quite new and already award-winning press that focussed initially on meeting a local need in Birmingham - a need for the vibrant poetry scene here in Brum to find a way to present itself to the poetry world via publication. Co-founded by Stuart Bartholomew and Amerah Saleh, it now publishes poets from all corners of the UK and beyond - poets that speak to the city's varied and energetic qualities and will contribute to its many poetic stories.

Added to this is a colourful pamphlet series, many featuring poets who have performed at our sister festival - and a poetry show series which captures the magic of longer poetry performance pieces by festival alumni such as Polarbear, Matt Abbott and Genevieve Carver.

The press has been voted Most Innovative Publisher at the Saboteur Awards, and has won the Publisher's Award for Poetry Pamphlets at the Michael Marks Awards.

Like the festival, we strive to think about poetry in inclusive ways and embrace the multiplicity of approaches towards this glorious art.

https://vervepoetrypress.com
@VervePoetryPres
mail@vervepoetrypress.com